Celebration Press Reading

Good Habits Great Readers™

Student Reader · Volume 1

■ ■ ■ ■ ■

CELEBRATION PRESS
Pearson Learning Group

Art and Design: Stephen Barth, Tricia Battipede, Alison O'Brien

Editorial: Adam Berkin, Linda Dorf, Alia Lesser, Cynthia Levinson, Linette Mathewson, Jennifer Van Der Heide

Inventory: Yvette Higgins

Marketing: Gina Konopinski-Jacobia

Production/Manufacturing: Lawrence Berkowitz, Alan Dalgleish, Karen Edmonds

Cover Illustrator: Lee White

Celebration Press Reading: Good Habits, Great Readers™

Flags
Text from *Flags* by Maureen Dockendorf and Sharon Jeroski. Copyright © 2005 Pearson Education, Inc., publishing as Celebration Press, an imprint of Pearson Learning Group. Compilation Copyright © 2005 Dorling Kindersley Ltd. All Rights Reserved.

The Many Faces of Masks
Text from *The Many Faces of Masks* by Cassie Welsh. Copyright © 2002 Pearson Education, Inc., publishing as Celebration Press, an imprint of Pearson Learning Group.

What Time Is It?
Text from *What Time Is It?* by Susan Ring. Copyright © 2005 Pearson Education, Inc., publishing as Celebration Press, an imprint of Pearson Learning Group. Compilation Copyright © 2005 Dorling Kindersley Ltd. All Rights Reserved.

Lady with the Lamp: The Florence Nightingale Story
Text Copyright © 2003 by Alan Trussell-Cullen

Every effort has been made to locate the copyright owners of material reprinted in this book. Omissions brought to our attention will be corrected in subsequent editions.

ISBN 1-4284-0439-2

Printed in the United States of America

10 V054 10

Celebration Press
Pearson Learning Group

1-800-321-3106
www.pearsonlearning.com
www.goodhabitsgreatreaders.com

Contents

Unit 2 Great Readers Make Sense of Text

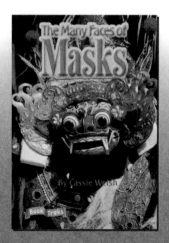

Unit 3 Great Readers Use What They Know

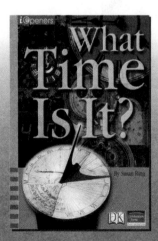

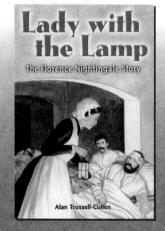

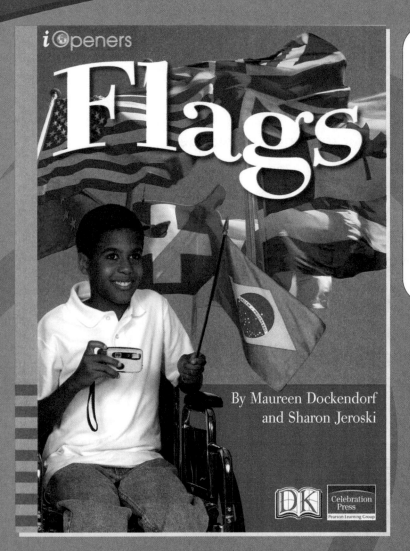

Words to Know

distinguish (p. 16): "to see the difference in"

independent (p. 22): "not controlled by others"

represented (p. 11): "stood for"

symbol (p. 10): "an object or a picture that represents something else"

Apply the Strategy

Lesson 1

Activating Prior Knowledge to Make Predictions

1. Look at the cover on page 6 and the contents page on page 9. Use the pages along with your prior knowledge to make predictions.
2. Record your predictions in a T-chart, labeling the left side *Prior Knowledge* and the right side *My Predictions*.

Prior Knowledge	My Predictions

Lesson 2

Using Text Structure to Make Predictions

1. Read page 10. Then look through pages 11–13, and use the text structure to predict what kind of information you might find in this chapter.
2. Repeat the process using pages 14–18.

3. Record your predictions on a concept web.
4. Read pages 10–18 to confirm or revise your predictions.

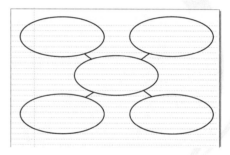

Lesson 3

Using Text Features to Make Predictions

1. Look through pages 19–25. Use the text features to make predictions.
2. Record your predictions in a T-chart, labeling the left side *Text Features* and the right side *My Predictions.*
3. Read pages 19–25 to confirm or revise your predictions.

Text Features	My Predictions

Contents

Flags Are Flying

A flag may look like a brightly colored piece of cloth, but it is actually much more than that. A flag can identify a nation. It can be an important symbol, standing for the beliefs, hopes, and dreams of the people who wave it. A flag can be used to rally people to a common cause. A flag can sometimes tell a story.

Flags are made to be seen, so most are large pieces of cloth that light breezes can blow.

Colors, patterns, and designs make each country's flag unique.

Ancient Flags

No one knows exactly what the first flag looked like or who used it. Many early societies used flags to identify themselves and to signal from a distance.

In ancient Egypt, warriors carried fans and carvings high on poles to identify themselves. Roman soldiers carried objects, often with small pieces of cloth attached, which identified their army units. In China and India, flags represented rulers or kings. In some cultures, flags carried such symbolism that if a flag fell in battle, it was as if the leader had been killed.

This ancient Egyptian pot shows a very early form of a flag on the top right.

Ancient Assyrians, from the area now called the Middle East, carried carved symbols on poles. These standards, which were carried into battle, were early forms of flags.

This is a modern reconstruction of an ancient Roman flag.

Flags of the Middle Ages

In the Middle Ages, cities, countries, and even powerful people used flags to identify themselves. Crosses, crescents, trefoils (symbols based on flowers or herbs with three leaves), lions, falcons, unicorns, and dragons were sewn onto colored fabric. These images were symbols that displayed information about the people who carried them. In battle, soldiers could recognize friends and enemies from a distance. If a city was captured, a flag was raised over its walls to identify the new ruler.

This medieval artwork shows a battle scene from the Hundred Years' War between France and England, which began in 1337. The artwork shows flags being carried into battle on horseback.

Pennants and Pennons

Flags come in many shapes, each with a special name. There are rectangular, triangular, and square flags. A few have tails or fringes. Pennants are flags that are much longer than they are wide. They are usually triangular. Pennons are also long and thin, but they often divide into two at the end.

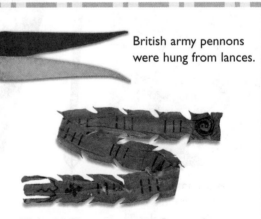

British army pennons were hung from lances.

This old Chinese pennant flew on boats.

Flags of Different Nations

Today, most of the world is divided into nations, and most nations have their own flags. Some of these flags were created hundreds of years ago. Others were designed recently. All the flags represent ideas or values that are important to that nation.

National flags are waved proudly at international gatherings to identify a country.

Many flags reflect their nation's past. They contain colors or patterns that represent important events in a nation's history. Others reflect the geography of a nation, its natural features, and its people. Some flags display symbols that stand for the beliefs, customs, and culture, or way of life, of the people.

The following chapters explore many different national flags. If you are unsure where a particular country is in the world, turn to pages 42 and 43 to find out.

National Flag Shapes

Kuwait

Nepal

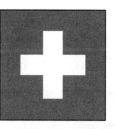

Switzerland

Most modern national flags are rectangular, such as Kuwait's flag. Nepal's flag is unusual because it's made of two joined triangles. Switzerland's flag is different from most flags because it is square.

Flags of Many Colors

National flags come in a rainbow of colors that are bold and easy to see from a distance. They are usually arranged in simple patterns that help people recognize the flag instantly. The colors represent things that are important to the people of each nation.

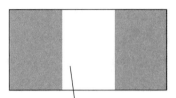

Nigeria

White represents peace and unity.

Colors of Nature

Green often symbolizes nature. The flag of Nigeria is green and white. A student, Michael Taiwo Akinkunmi, designed this flag to honor the fields and forests of his country. In 1958, his flag was chosen from almost 3,000 entries in a competition.

Brazil also has a flag with green on it, representing the lush rain forests covering much of that country. Yellow or gold can represent many things. Ukraine's flag has a yellow stripe that represents wheat fields.

Brazil is home to the Amazon rain forest.

Brazil

The yellow diamond represents Brazil's mineral resources.

Ukraine

Blue represents the sky.

Yellow represents wheat fields.

Many island countries, such as the Bahamas, have blue on their flags to represent the sea that surrounds them. Other countries use blue to represent the sky, whereas others see blue as a color of peace.

Red may represent blood, or the sacrifice people made to fight for their country's independence. Red is also used to represent a number of different political or religious beliefs.

White sometimes represents ice or snow. That is its meaning on the flag of Finland, a country in the far north. However, white also represents ideals such as hope, love, freedom, or peace.

Often, you need to know the story behind a flag to discover what a color symbolizes. The five colors in the flag of Seychelles have symbolic meanings.

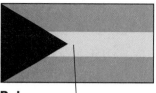

Bahamas

Yellow represents the sandy beaches of the Bahamas.

Finland

White represents snow and ice.

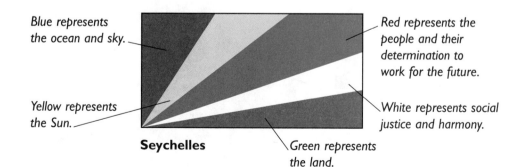

Blue represents the ocean and sky.

Yellow represents the Sun.

Seychelles

Green represents the land.

Red represents the people and their determination to work for the future.

White represents social justice and harmony.

Historic Colors

Some flag colors tell a story about a country's history. In 1785, the king of Spain adopted red and yellow for the national flag. This color combination was not used by any other nation, so it was easy to distinguish Spain's ships from those of other countries.

Spain

The flag of the Netherlands also tells a story of its history. More than 400 years ago, Spain controlled the Netherlands. Prince William of Orange, one of the Dutch leaders, raised an army to help drive the Spanish out. After winning their freedom, the people of the Netherlands adopted an orange, white, and blue flag, similar to Prince William's personal flag. Eventually, the orange stripe was changed to red. To this day, the Netherlands' flag honors William's place in the country's history.

William of Orange

Netherlands

The Netherlands' flag is a tricolor, which means that it has three equal-sized stripes of three colors.

The French flag is also red, white, and blue. Although the colors are the same as the Dutch flag, the history of this flag is different. White was the color of the kings of France, while blue and red were the colors of the capital city of Paris.

France

In the late 1700s, many people in Paris were starving, while the king and members of the ruling class used France's wealth for themselves. The French people began a revolution to rid France of the king. In 1792, the people overthrew the king, and a new French government was started. Since then, red, white, and blue have represented liberty to people around the world.

The French Revolution began on July 14, 1789, when the people of Paris stormed the Bastille prison.

Some nations chose their flag colors or designs because they were inspired by other nations. The red, white, and blue horizontal stripes of the Russian Federation flag is an example of this. Peter the Great, an emperor of Russia who lived from 1672 to 1725, traveled to the Netherlands and brought its ideas back to Russia. He started schools, built a navy, and even made people dress differently. Although the colors of the Dutch flag had been used for many years, Peter the Great made the horizontal stripes a feature of his own nation's flag.

Paraguay's flag is also red, white, and blue. During the nineteenth century, Paraguay fought for independence from Spain. Inspired by the French Revolution, the people of Paraguay used the colors of the French flag.

Peter the Great

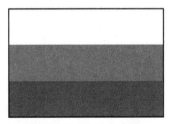

Russian Federation

Paraguay

The colors of Paraguay's flag were taken from the French flag. There is a different emblem on the front and the back of the flag.

State Arms on front of flag

Treasury Seal on back of flag

The Symbols on Flags

Simple bands of color make up the design of many national flags. Other flags have special symbols. These symbols represent important natural features, religious or historic ideas, or cultural traditions.

Symbols of Nature

Lebanon has a cedar tree on its flag. Known as the cedar of Lebanon, this tree has been an important part of Lebanon's history. It provided wood and cedar oil for many ancient civilizations.

The flag of Kiribati, an island nation in the Pacific Ocean, has six wavy bands of blue and white on it. These bands represent the ocean waves. A Sun symbol rises from the waves. Above the Sun is a frigate bird.

The frigate bird is found all over the Pacific.

Lebanon   cedar tree

Kiribati

Stars

Many flags have stars on them. Sometimes these stars represent specific stars or constellations. Flags of some countries in the southern hemisphere, including Australia, New Zealand, and Papua New Guinea, feature a constellation known as the Southern Cross. For centuries, sailors sailing in the southern oceans have used this constellation to guide them.

On Cape Verde's flag, the ten stars represent the ten main islands that make up the country.

Southern Cross Constellation

bird of paradise

Papua New Guinea

Cape Verde

The islands of Cape Verde lie in the Atlantic Ocean, off the coast of west Africa.

New Zealand

The Southern Cross constellation on New Zealand's flag forms a diamond shape.

China

Stars can represent ideas as well. China's flag has five stars. One star is larger than the others and represents communism, a form of government. The Communist Party is the country's governing body. The smaller stars represent groups of people in the country, such as workers and peasants.

The flag of Guinea-Bissau has a black star. This represents freedom and respect for African people.

The star is also a symbol that shows the important role religion plays in many cultures. A star and crescent Moon can be found on flags from many nations where Islam is an important religion. The cross, a Christian symbol, can also be found on many flags.

People in China often hang flags from their apartment blocks to celebrate Chinese National Day.

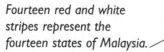

Guinea-Bissau

A gold star and crescent Moon are traditional symbols for Muslim people.

Fourteen red and white stripes represent the fourteen states of Malaysia.

Malaysia

Historic Symbols

Many flags tell the history of a country. Some designs represent an important event, such as when a country became independent. Others use symbols from much earlier cultures and times. Argentina's flag does both.

Argentina

The symbol of the Sun at the center of Argentina's flag celebrates the culture of the Incas, Native Americans of Peru, Argentina, and other countries of modern-day South America. The Sun of May on the Argentinean flag represents pride in the Inca culture and also celebrates Argentina's independence from Spain in May, 1816.

The Sun of May symbol is part of Argentina's flag.

Early civilizations are represented on other flags, too. The Cambodian flag displays the image of Angkor Wat, an ancient temple built almost 1,000 years ago.

Cambodia

Angkor Wat, a temple in Cambodia, is depicted on the nation's flag.

Mexico

Arms of Mexico

This Aztec stone carving has been dated to 1325. The carving shows the eagle of Aztec legend.

Mexico's flag has an image of an eagle sitting on a cactus eating a snake. This image celebrates a legend of the Aztecs, who are also native peoples of the Americas.

Some flags show the traditional weapons of nations of the past. Swaziland's flag has the image of a shield, a staff, and two spears. The shield and staff are decorated with the images of feathers from local birds. These symbols represent the fight for independence as well as the traditions of the people of Swaziland.

Flags that celebrate people of the past show how much countries everywhere value their history.

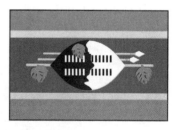

Swaziland

Swazi shields are usually made from cow hides.

Poles are put through rows of slits to make shields rigid.

A symbol representing a yurt is found on the flag of Kyrgyzstan.

Some people in Kyrgyzstan still live in yurts.

Kyrgyzstan

The Sun symbol has forty rays. Each ray represents one of the forty Kyrgyz tribes.

Cultural traditions are also represented on flags. From ancient times, the Kyrgyz (KIR-gihz) people were nomads. They moved from place to place in search of grazing land for their animals. The Kyrgyz people lived in yurts, or felt tents. Though life has changed for most Kyrgyz, the yurt is still an important part of their culture. It is represented within a yellow Sun symbol on the flag of Kyrgyzstan (kir-gih-STAN).

Turkmenistan has a long tradition of carpet-making. People weave the complex patterns of the carpets by hand.

Turkmenistan

A stripe on the flag of Turkmenistan represents traditional carpet designs.

Japan

The Sun rises over Wakayama's rocky coastline in Japan.

Japan's flag, a white field with a red circle in the center, celebrates nature, history, and religion. *Japan* means "Land of the Rising Sun" and the red circle represents the Sun. The emperor of Japan comes from a family that traditionally was said to have descended from a Sun goddess and the red Sun symbol celebrates that connection, as well.

Circles don't always represent the Sun. The red circle on the flag from Bangladesh represents the blood lost in its fight for independence. The yellow circle on the flag from Palau represents the Moon and stands for peace. The people of Palau believe that the full Moon is the best time for harvesting, fishing, and celebration.

Bangladesh

Palau

Apply the Strategy

Lesson 1

Asking Text-Explicit Questions

1. Read pages 28–31, and think of text-explicit questions.
2. Record questions and answers in a T-chart, labeling the left side *Text-Explicit Questions* and the right side *Answers*.

Text-Explicit Questions	Answers

Lesson 2

Asking Text-Implicit Questions

1. Skim pages 28–31, and think of text-implicit questions. Use clues from the text and your own knowledge and experience to answer the questions.
2. Record questions, clues, and answers in a three-column chart, labeling the columns *Text-Implicit Question, Clues and Knowledge,* and *Answers*.

Text-Implicit Question	Clues and Knowledge	Answers

Lesson 3

Generating Questions Throughout Reading

1. Read pages 32–34, and think of text-explicit and text-implicit questions.
2. Record questions in a T-chart, labeling the left side *Text-Explicit Questions* and the right side *Text-Implicit Questions*.

Text-Explicit Questions	Text-Implicit Questions

Changing Flags

Nations change over time. Their borders can move because of new agreements between countries or war. Different governments come to power because of new laws or revolution. When nations change, their flags may change, too.

Afghanistan
A new flag was adopted by Afghanistan after the ruling Taliban fell from power in 2001.

The Union Jack

The United Kingdom is made up of England, Northern Ireland, Scotland, and Wales. Its flag, the Union Flag, also known as the Union Jack, is a combination of the flags of three of the four countries.

In 1603, King James of Scotland became king of England, too. Each country kept its own flag, but the new kingdom flew flags from its ships that combined both designs. In the 1800s, Ireland became part of the United Kingdom. One of its flags at the time, a red diagonal cross on white, was added to the United Kingdom's flag. Wales was united with England in the 1500s, but its flag design, which includes a red dragon, is not part of the Union Jack.

United Kingdom
A "jack" is a small flag that is flown on the bow, or front, mast of a ship. In the 1600s, an early version of the Union Jack was flown from ships.

The Union Jack and Other Nations

For many centuries, the United Kingdom explored the world and established settlements, or colonies, on different continents. Today, most of these colonies are independent nations. Some, such as Canada, South Africa, and India, have flags based on traditional designs or symbols that were important before British rule. Other nations, such as Australia, New Zealand, and Fiji, continue to include a Union Jack in one corner.

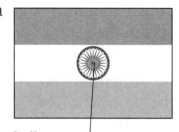

India

Dharma Chakra (wheel of law)

Canada became divided over the issue of a new national flag in the early 1960s. Canadian Prime Minister Lester B. Pearson called for a new flag to be designed with a symbol specific to Canada.

Fiji

The Union Jack represents Fiji's historical links with the United Kingdom.

The maple tree, with its sweet sap and valuable wood, has been important to people living in Canada for hundreds of years. When Canada introduced its new national flag in 1965, a red maple leaf was included in the middle white band. Red and white are the national colors of Canada.

maple leaf

Canada

Australia was once part of the British Empire. Its flag has a Union Jack in the canton, or the upper corner nearest the flagpole. Beneath the Union Jack is a seven-pointed star that represents the six states and the territories that make up Australia. The Southern Cross constellation appears on the fly, or the outer edge of the flag.

Different groups of people within a country often have their own flag to represent themselves. The original inhabitants, or the indigenous peoples, of Australia are the Aboriginal and Torres Strait Islander peoples. They officially adopted their black, gold, and red flag in 1972.

Australia

Aboriginal flag

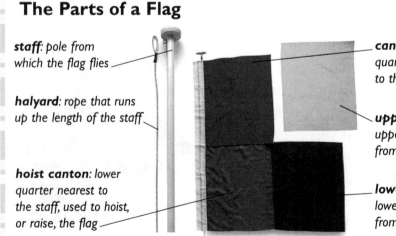

Kathy Freeman, an indigenous Australian athlete, celebrated a victory with both the Australian and Aboriginal flags.

The Parts of a Flag

staff: pole from which the flag flies

halyard: rope that runs up the length of the staff

hoist canton: lower quarter nearest to the staff, used to hoist, or raise, the flag

canton: upper quarter nearest to the staff

upper fly canton: upper quarter farthest from the staff

lower fly canton: lower quarter farthest from the staff

The flag of the United States also used to include a Union Jack. This flag, known as the Continental Colors or the Grand Union flag, had thirteen red and white stripes that represented the union of the thirteen original British colonies.

As the American colonies moved toward independence from the United Kingdom, different flags were used for the new country. In 1777, the Continental Congress passed the first Flag Act. This act created a flag that had thirteen stripes, alternating between red and white, and a blue field with thirteen stars. This was the first version of the Stars and Stripes.

Although no one knows for sure, most historians believe that Francis Hopkinson designed this version of the Stars and Stripes flag. There is a legend that Betsy Ross, a seamstress in Philadelphia made the first flag, but most facts do not support this story.

The United States flag kept changing as more states joined the union. At first, a stripe and a star was added for each new state. Later it was decided to keep thirteen stripes, for the original thirteen colonies. Stars were added to show how many states there are. The last star was added in 1960 when Hawaii became a state.

The Union Jack was a symbol of the colonists' loyalty to the United Kingdom.

Grand Union flag

first Stars and Stripes

Fifty stars represent the number of states in the US today.

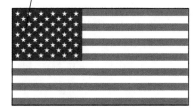

United States

International Flags

People say the world is getting smaller. It is easier to travel from country to country than ever before. Citizens of one country do business with people from other countries every day, and it is common for people to work or travel in other countries.

Uniting Nations

Many international organizations have formed to help different nations interact. These organizations have flags to identify themselves and their member countries.

United Nations (UN)

The United Nations (UN) is an international organization made up of many nations from all around the world. It was organized to keep the world peaceful and to help resolve emergencies and disagreements between nations.

The flag of the United Nations is pale blue, which stands for peace. The flag shows a white map of the world surrounded by olive branches, ancient symbols of peace and harmony.

The UN's headquarters in New York, United States, has flags from member nations flying outside.

Some international flags represent the union of countries in specific regions of the world. The European Union (EU) is an international organization made up of countries in Europe. The countries cooperate economically, reduce trade barriers, and most use the same currency.

European Union (EU)

The Arab League represents Middle Eastern countries such as Saudia Arabia, Kuwait, and Lebanon. A gold chain on the Arab League's green flag represents the unity of the countries.

Arab League

The Association of Southeast Asian Nations (ASEAN) encourages countries such as Singapore, Malaysia, and Thailand to work together. Its flag includes a design representing ten rice stalks. Each stalk represents one of the ten member nations. The blue background of the flag represents peace and stability.

Association of Southeast Asian Nations (ASEAN)

The Caribbean Community and Common Market (CARICOM) was founded in 1973. Countries that are members include the Bahamas and Jamaica.

Dark blue represents the sea.

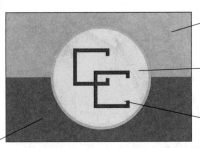

Light blue represents the sky.

The yellow circle represents the Sun.

The black letters are the initials of the Caribbean Community.

Caribbean Community and Common Market (CARICOM)

More International Flags

The Red Cross and the Red Crescent flags represent international groups that bring health care and emergency relief to people all over the world. The flags are symbols of peace and care, but they are also signals. The organization's workers are often in dangerous locations, including war zones. The flags signal that the workers have no part in the conflict.

The flag of the Olympic Games displays five interlocking rings representing the union of athletes from five parts of the world—Africa, the Americas, Asia, Australia, and Europe.

Some flags don't relate to an organization, but have meanings that are understood worldwide. A plain white flag often means truce, or surrender. A yellow flag warns of disease.

Red Crescent

Red Cross

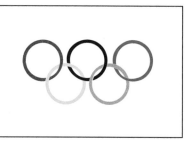

Olympic Games

Jolly Roger

A white skull and crossed bones or swords on a black background is familiar as the flag of pirate ships.

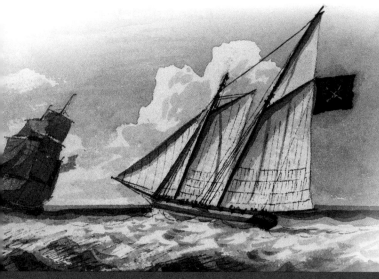

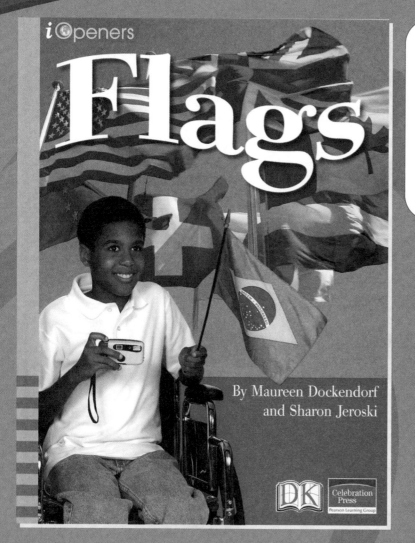

iOpeners

Flags

By Maureen Dockendorf
and Sharon Jeroski

DK Celebration Press
Pearson Learning Group

Words to Know

citizens (p. 39): "people who are members of a country"

respect (p. 39): "honor"

spectators (p. 41): "people who watch or observe"

Apply the Strategy

Lesson 1

Generating Questions to Anticipate Events or Information

1. Read pages 39–43. Pause after the first paragraph on page 39 to ask questions that the text has made you wonder about.
2. Record your questions in a T-chart, labeling the left side *Questions* and the right side *Predictions/Answers*.
3. As you continue to read, pose other questions and record them in your chart.

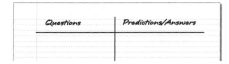

Lesson 2

Questioning the Author

1. Skim pages 39–43. Think of questions you would like to ask the author.
2. Record questions and possible responses in a T-chart, labeling the left side *Questions to the Authors* and the right side *Possible Author Response*.

Questions to the Authors	Possible Author Response

Lesson 3

Asking Questions to Resolve Confusion

1. Skim pages 39–41.
2. Record questions about things that you are not sure of in a T-chart, labeling the left side *Questions* and the right side *Solutions*.
3. Work with a partner to resolve your questions and add solutions to your chart.

Questions	Solutions

Flag Customs and Traditions

Citizens of all nations treat their flags with respect. In fact, most countries have laws to ensure that they do so. Respecting the flag means different things in different countries, however.

This Icelandic flag is flying at half-mast, a sign of respect and sorrow about the death of an important person.

Respecting the Flag

Citizens in some countries believe the flag should not be dipped in salute to any person. It definitely should never touch the ground. In other countries, however, dipping a flag is a common sign of respect.

In some countries, it is also disrespectful to write on the flag. In other countries, this is not considered disrespectful at all. For example, in Argentina, 750 people who gave money to help World War I soldiers signed their names on a decorative Argentinean flag.

During World War II, some Japanese soldiers carried national flags into battle that had prayers and good wishes from their families written on them. The prayers were never written over the red Sun symbol.

Flags in Exploration

It is a tradition to erect a flag to mark a great feat of exploration. Mountaineers, astronauts, and adventurers have left their flag at their final destination, wherever that may be.

The erection of a flag does not mean that a particular nation owns the place. Roald Amundsen planted the Norwegian flag on the South Pole on December 14, 1911, but this doesn't mean that the South Pole belongs to Norway.

The flags of many countries fly at the South Pole. They represent explorers who reached the Pole.

There is no atmosphere on the Moon—so no wind. Flags in space are often specially wired or hung from a horizontal bar to look like they are fluttering in the breeze.

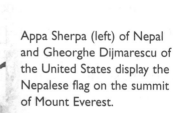

Appa Sherpa (left) of Nepal and Gheorghe Dijmarescu of the United States display the Nepalese flag on the summit of Mount Everest.

Flags and Fun

Flags are important national symbols, but that doesn't stop them from being fun. They are flown at festivals all over the world, giving people the chance to celebrate their own country and to learn about others.

Flags can decorate everything from clothes and bags to mugs and plates. Sometimes the whole flag design is printed onto objects, and other times just the colors are borrowed to represent a particular nation.

Flags play a huge role in international sporting events. Spectators cheer on their national team and show support by waving their nation's flag.

These Norwegian soccer fans have painted their faces with the colors of Norway's flag.

At this National Festival of Youth in Burundi, school groups perform traditional dances and songs under their national flag (center).

The tallest supported flagpole in the world is in North Korea. It soars 525 feet into the sky.

Flags of the World

There are more than 190 countries in the world, and all of them have their own national flag. Here, we show the location of the countries whose flags we have explored in this book.

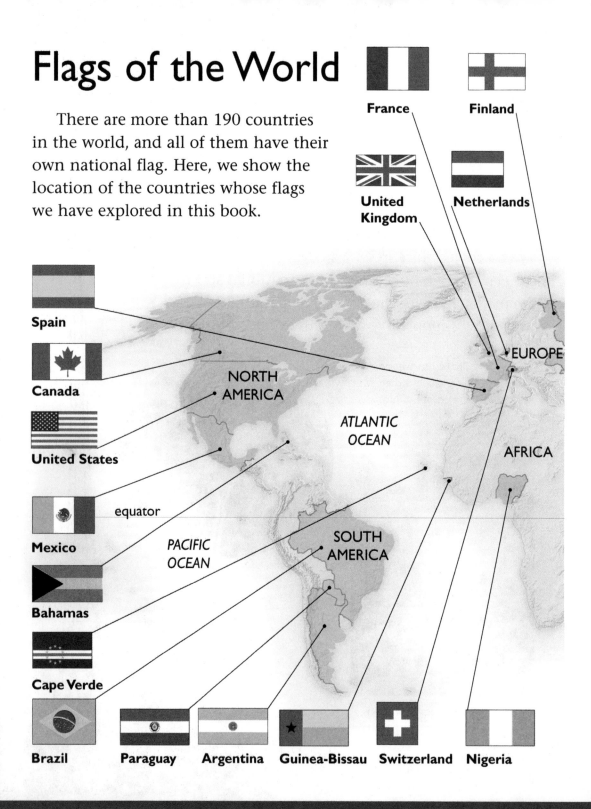

France

Finland

United Kingdom

Netherlands

Spain

Canada

United States

Mexico

Bahamas

Cape Verde

Brazil

Paraguay

Argentina

Guinea-Bissau

Switzerland

Nigeria

EUROPE

NORTH AMERICA

ATLANTIC OCEAN

AFRICA

PACIFIC OCEAN

equator

SOUTH AMERICA

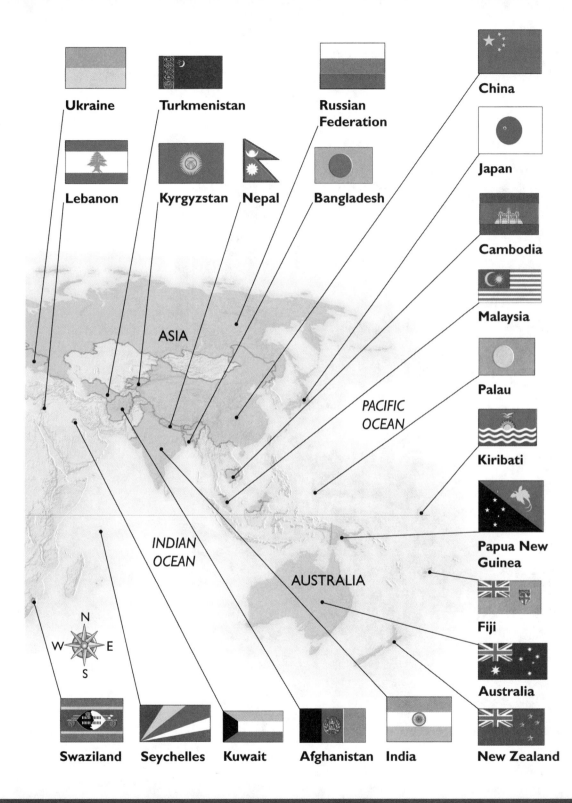

Ukraine

Turkmenistan

Russian Federation

China

Lebanon

Kyrgyzstan

Nepal

Bangladesh

Japan

ASIA

Cambodia

Malaysia

PACIFIC OCEAN

Palau

Kiribati

INDIAN OCEAN

Papua New Guinea

AUSTRALIA

N
W E
S

Fiji

Australia

Swaziland

Seychelles

Kuwait

Afghanistan

India

New Zealand

Clarifying
Great Readers Make Sense of Text

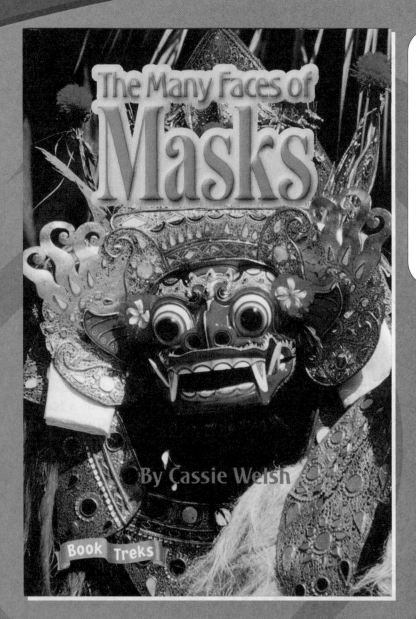

Apply the Strategy

Lesson 1

Using Discussion to Clarify

1. Read pages 47–49.
2. Record words or ideas that you are not sure of in a T-chart, labeling the left side *Things That I Don't Understand* and the right side *Clarifying the Text*.
3. Work with a partner to clarify the text.

Things That I Don't Understand	Clarifying the Text

What to Clarify	How to Solve Them

Lesson 3

Activating Prior Knowledge to Clarify

1. Read pages 50–53.
2. Record confusing concepts in a T-chart, labeling the left side *Things to Clarify* and the right side *Prior Knowledge*.
3. Work with a partner to discuss how your prior knowledge and experiences can help you resolve the confusion.

Things to Clarify	Prior Knowledge

Lesson 2

Reading Ahead and Rereading to Clarify

1. Skim pages 47–49.
2. Record words or concepts that you don't understand and your ideas for resolving them in a T-chart, labeling the left side *What to Clarify* and the right side *How to Solve Them*.

Contents

Introduction

Masks have been made and used for different purposes for thousands of years.

If someone asked you to define *mask*, what would you say? You might say that a mask is a face covering or disguise worn with costumes at celebrations or parties. You might say that it is something that protects the face during work or in battle. Or you might say it is part of a costume that actors wear.

If you answered in any of these ways, you would be correct. In fact, masks have been used throughout human history for many different purposes and have played a role in almost every culture.

Mask Faces

Masks are as different as faces and can be made of wood, metal, cloth, leather, clay, or other materials. They can be **anthropomorphic**—having human features. Or they can be **theriomorphic**—having animal features.

You could probably make a simple mask with eyes, nose, and lips out of cardboard in a few minutes. More complex masks may be decorated with finely carved patterns, feathers, jewels, or shells. Skilled **artisans** often take months to create such masks.

These two Indonesian men are painting masks to be worn in a Balinese dance.

Way Back When...

Masks have existed for thousands and thousands of years. The first masks were probably animal masks that people wore while praying before the hunt or while hunting. People made these masks between about 40,000 and 10,000 B.C. None of these masks exists today, probably because they were made of animal skins or other materials that do not last.

Several ancient cave paintings have masks in them. **Archaeologists** have found prehistoric drawings of humans wearing animal masks in many areas of the world, including the Sahara Desert in Africa and in North America, Spain, and France.

The cave paintings found at Les Trois Frères, a cave in southern France, are some of the oldest art showing masks in human culture. This cave contains hundreds of paintings of humans, animals, and humans wearing animal heads, which are at least 10,000 years old! The best-known figure in the cave paintings, the Sorcerer, is a man wearing a stag's head. A stag is a male deer. Many archaeologists believe that the human figure in this drawing was wearing a stag mask to prepare himself for hunting.

Stories, Ceremonies, and Festivals

Native Americans of the Northwest Coast carved colorful wooden masks of animal characters such as Wolf, Raven, and Bear. They wore the masks at many festivals, including **potlatches**.

At a potlatch, special events like marriages were announced, and dancers performed special dances wearing animal masks. The dances told traditional stories about the animal characters. These stories, hundreds of years old, were performed and passed down from generation to generation.

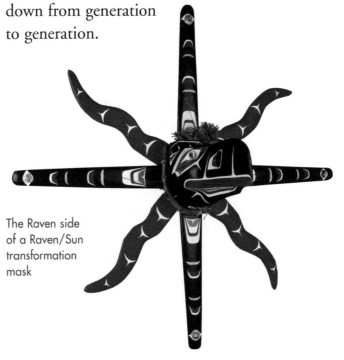

The Raven side of a Raven/Sun transformation mask

The Sun side of a Raven/Sun transformation mask

Many of these dance stories are about Raven, a clever trickster. The mask above tells the story about the time that Raven tried to steal light from the Sun.

The mask is the same mask you saw on page 50. It is a **transformation mask**. The Raven side folds back and reveals the Sun. Its movable parts allowed its wearer to "change" from one character to another to better act out the story. These masks are still important to the Native Americans of the Northwest Coast. They help keep their ancient stories alive.

Across the Pacific Ocean on the island of Bali, Indonesia, masks are still used to perform stories that are thousands of years old. Some of these stories came from India more than 2,000 years ago. The Balinese wear highly decorated costumes and special masks as they tell the stories by performing dances.

Masks play a central role in the dances. The dancers' masks and costumes show which characters they are and whether they are heroes or villains. Some masks are so important that only certain dancers are allowed to wear them, and only certain mask makers are allowed to make them, after sacred ceremonies.

Two of the most important masks in Balinese culture are Rangda and the Barong. The Rangda mask is especially detailed—and frightening. Most Rangda masks have long tusks and a very long red and gold tongue. They also have extremely long, tangled hair attached to them. This hair, made of horsehair and other stiff fibers, helps to make Rangda appear especially wicked. Rangda represents evil.

In contrast, the Barong is a creature who represents good. Don't let its pointy teeth and lionish grin fool you! The Barong dance story tells of the Barong's encounter with Rangda. In the dance the two creatures battle each other in a forest.

Mask makers carve much of the Barong mask from wood and then attach decorations to it made of feathers, gold-painted leather, and tiny mirrors. They put a great deal of care into every detail. They must cut small designs into the golden crown. The movable jaw must be just the right size so that the wearer can move it with his own jaw. The mask makers must carefully sew each mirror into the leather. Making a mask like this can take up to four months!

A dancer wearing a Barong mask

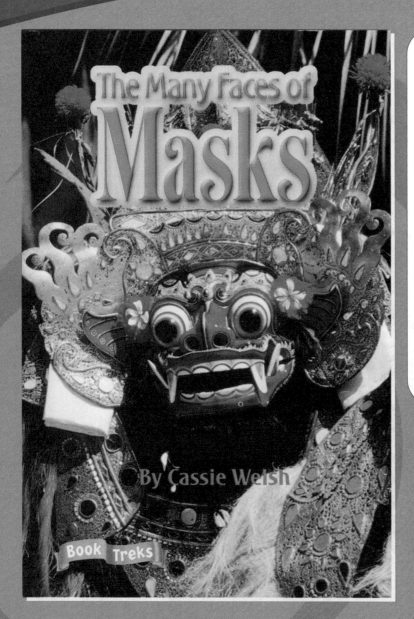

executed (p. 57): "put to death"

inherits (p. 66): "obtains something passed down from an ancestor"

missionaries (p. 58): "people sent by a church to foreign countries to teach, heal, and spread religious practices"

papier-mâché (p. 57): "lightweight, strong material made mostly of paper mixed with glue used for shaping masks"

Apply the Strategy

Lesson 1

Pausing to Paraphrase as You Read

1. Read pages 56–60. Use sticky notes to mark the most important ideas and pause every so often to paraphrase what you have read.
2. Record your paraphrased statements in a list, labeling it *Masks*.

• *Masks*

Lesson 3

Combining Related Information

1. Read pages 65–66, and look for ways to group ideas.
2. Record related ideas and summary sentences in a T-chart, labeling the left side *Related Ideas* and the right side *Summary*.

Related Ideas	*Summary*

Lesson 2

Distinguishing Between Main Ideas and Details to Create a Summary

1. Read pages 61–64. Identify the main ideas and supporting details.
2. Write a summary of what you read.

• *Masks on Stage*

The Carnival of Oruro is a pre-Easter festival with brightly costumed masked dancers, music, street dramas, and parades.

In many places in the world, people perform masked story-dances for special festivals. In some cultures these festivals are annual events that attract thousands of people. Often such folk festivals take place in the center of town. Masked dancers parade through the streets, acting out stories and folk tales important to that culture. The Carnival of Oruro, in Bolivia, South America, is one such festival. It begins on the Saturday before Lent, the Christian religious season before Easter.

Dancers usually wear masks made of papier-mâché or plaster of Paris. These materials are molded over wire frames and then painted. The materials absorb the paint easily, so the masks can have even more brilliant colors than a painted wooden mask. Papier-mâché masks are also more lightweight than wood or metal masks, which makes it easier for the dancers to wear them for long periods of time.

During the Carnival of Oruro, the masked dancers perform several different kinds of stories. These stories, though partly made up, still tell a great deal about the history of the Bolivian people.

Many Bolivians today have both Spanish and Inca ancestors. The dance-stories allow them to explore their past from both sides of their heritage.

One dance-story tells of the Inca people and their defeat by the Spanish **conquistadors**. The great Inca Empire stretched across western South America in parts of present-day Bolivia, Ecuador, Chile, Peru, and Argentina before the Spanish arrived in the 1500s.

The Inca dance performed at the Carnival tells of the legendary last Inca ruler, Atahualpa (ah tuh WAHL puh). The Spanish explorer Francisco Pizarro captured and executed him. The Inca dance celebrates Atahualpa's bravery.

The Inca dance, however, is not the only masked dance performed at the Carnival of Oruro. The diablada, or devil dance, is one of the best-known dances in many parts of South America. Some of the most colorful and interesting masks are worn by the diablada dancers. These masks are often decorated with snakes, toads, and lizards.

Carnival celebrations began in Europe during the Middle Ages, about A.D. 500–1500, as religious festivals. People in Germany, the United States, Spain, and Mexico today still use masks to celebrate and tell stories during their Carnival festivals.

As in Bolivia, Carnival in Mexico began after the Spanish conquest in the 1500s. When Spanish missionaries arrived in Mexico, they used masked plays and stories to try to persuade the native people to accept the Spanish people's beliefs. These masked plays were based on plays that were very popular in Europe at this time.

The missionaries also introduced Mexico to the festival of Carnival. At that time in Europe, Carnival was a popular time of celebration before a period of deep religious thought and fasting. In Mexico, the native peoples adopted much of the new celebration, but they also changed it. They created their own types of masks and added their own stories and dances.

One such Mexican dance, *la danza de los catrines* (lah DAHN zuh day lohs cuh TREE nays)—the dance of the dandies, pokes fun at the wealthy landowners of ages past. The masks worn for this dance are extremely lifelike. Although the mask wearers look through slits in the eyebrows of the mask, they can still blink and wink at people. How can they do this? These masks have glass eyes with false eyelashes. The mask wearer opens and closes the eyes using a string attached to a special spring.

Dancers wearing Catrin masks

You are probably familiar with a Carnival festival celebrated each year in some places in the United States—Mardi Gras. *Mardi gras* means "fat Tuesday" in French. This name indicates that Carnival is, for some people, a day of celebration before a period of fasting. People usually ate a great deal on this Tuesday.

Today the most famous Mardi Gras celebration in the United States takes place in New Orleans, Louisiana. Mardi Gras differs quite a bit from Carnivals in Mexico and Bolivia. During Mardi Gras, people do not usually perform traditional dances. Instead, **krewes**, or private groups of parade participants, organize and pay for parades and parties. They help choose themes for Mardi Gras parades and decorate the elaborate floats accordingly.

They also choose costumes and masks that reflect the parade's theme. Sometimes krewes wear masks that represent historical figures. Other times they wear masks that represent ancient heroes from Greek, Roman, and Egyptian myths. Some people wear simple plain black or white masks to disguise their faces, as they would at a masquerade ball. These different kinds of masks show that Mardi Gras is really a melting pot of many cultures, much like the United States itself.

Masks on Stage

Perhaps one of the most popular uses of masks in European and other Western cultures has been by actors in the theater. Masks aren't often used in performances today. But their past importance to the theater is clear in the symbol used for drama—two simple masks, side by side, one frowning and one smiling. The masks stand for tragedy and comedy.

The use of masks in the theater goes back to ancient Greece and Rome. Unlike the gold masks of ancient Egypt, these masks no longer exist. However, we know from paintings that Greek masks exaggerated the features and were probably made of leather or canvas.

The Greek theater masks showed basic expressions such as anger, happiness, or sadness. They also contained a megaphone that amplified the actors' voices, so that everyone in the theater could hear. The large size of the masks and the amplifier were extremely useful in the large outdoor theaters of ancient Greece.

Masks were also used in plays during the Middle Ages and the Renaissance (1300s to 1600s). During the Middle Ages, mystery plays, based on stories from the Bible, were especially popular. There were masked demons, dragons, and the devil. The masks used for these plays were usually made of papier-mâché and were very effective. Some of these masks even thrilled audiences with special effects, such as blowing smoke and fire.

During the Renaissance in Italy, a form of theater called the **commedia dell'arte** (koh MAY dee ah del LAHR tay) became popular. The term means "comedy of art" in Italian. All of these plays were comedies. Actors wore special masks that represented well-known types of characters. The actors wearing these masks "became" these characters and improvised, or made stories up during the performance.

This painting shows masked characters performing in the commedia dell'arte.

One popular character was Harlequin, a comic servant who was very clever. He was an acrobat and wore a catlike mask and colorful patched clothing.

The commedia dell'arte lost popularity in the 1700s. But historians today think that the mime, the clown, and the masquerade mask have all been influenced by the commedia dell'arte theater.

In Japan today, actors perform the still-popular masked **Noh drama**. Noh drama began in the early 1300s and is traditionally performed only by men.

For these dramas there are about 125 types of mask faces—men and women, young and old, and imaginary creatures. The masks are painted in traditional colors to show the character's nature—for example, red for the hero and black for the villain. A white mask is used to show a corrupt ruler.

A mask maker, or **tenka-ichi**, carefully carves each mask. It is made of wood and covered with plaster and a lacquer that gives it a glossy glaze. This light-reflecting glaze helps create the illusion that the mask is changing expressions as the actor moves his head.

A Japanese actor in costume and mask during a Noh drama

The Mask Maker's Process

In some cultures the mask makers are specially trained and are important figures in the community. They are often seen primarily as craftspersons. In some African villages, for example, mask makers are also blacksmiths who make the tools used for mask carving as well. They usually learn the craft of mask making from their fathers or become **apprentices** to skilled mask makers. As an apprentice they learn the secrets of mask making and how to use the tools of the trade.

In some cultures, mask makers must gather materials for their masks. Certain masks can only be made of certain materials. For example, Balinese mask makers make Rangda masks only from the *kepuh-rangdu* or *pule* tree. Mask makers often obtain these special materials themselves or entrust the work to a trusted member of their community.

Once the mask makers have the necessary materials, they begin work. Plaster masks need to be molded, dried, and painted. Metal masks must often be melted and then shaped and decorated. Wooden masks need to be shaped, carved, and painted.

The tools that mask makers use to create their masks are extremely important to them, much like a lucky tennis racket might be to a tennis player. For example, in some African cultures, mask makers carve wooden masks with a special tool called an adz, which has a thin, curved blade. Often a young mask maker inherits this tool from another mask maker. The young mask maker then carries on a tradition by using that same adz.

This African woodcarver is using an adz like the ones mask makers use.

Glossary

archaeologist a scientist who studies the people and culture of ancient times by studying ancient objects, such as drawings or pottery

artisan a skilled craftsperson

apprentice a person who learns a trade by assisting an experienced craftsperson

anthropomorphic having human features

commedia dell'arte a form of comic theater popular during the Renaissance, which featured improvisation and masked characters

conquistadors Spanish conquerors of Mexico and Peru in the 1500s

krewe a private group who organize and pay for the parades and parties during Mardi Gras

Moshambwooy a mask that represents the Kuba people's ancestor Woot

Noh drama a popular Japanese masked drama that began in the 1300s

potlatch a Northwest Coast Native American festival at which a family gave gifts and announced marriages or other special events. The hosts and guests performed masked dances.

tenka-ichi a Japanese Noh mask maker

theriomorphic having animal features

transformation mask a complex Northwest Coast Native American mask, which can change from one animal or character to another (for example, one side might be a sun and the other, a raven)

By Susan Ring

Words to Know

crescent (p. 77): "the thin, curved shape of the Moon when it looks small"

gibbous (p. 77): "the shape of the Moon when it is more than half full but less than full"

waning (p. 77): "the decreasing visible shape of the Moon after the full moon"

waxing (p. 77): "the increasing visible shape of the Moon before the full moon"

Apply the Strategy

Lesson 1

Thinking About What You Know Before Reading

1. Look at the cover of *What Time Is It?* on page 68. Think about what you know about time.
2. Record your ideas on a concept web.

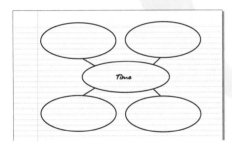

Lesson 2

Considering Your Purpose for Reading

1. Think about the reasons someone might have for reading a book about time.
2. Record your purposes for reading and your background knowledge of time in a T-chart, labeling the left side *My Purpose for Reading* and the right side *What I Know*.

My Purpose for Reading	What I Know

Lesson 3

Previewing to Activate Background Knowledge

1. Preview pages 71–93. Use the information you gather to narrow down the background knowledge you'll need to understand the text.
2. Modify your concept web from Lesson 1.
3. Discuss your changes with a partner.

Contents

Keeping Track of Time

What time is it? Most people ask that question many times a day. People don't want to be late for class or early for a visit. They don't want to wake up too early or go to bed too late. Favorite television shows or celebrations usually happen at a certain time or on certain days. Clocks and calendars help people keep track of what time and day it is.

Ancient peoples looked to the seasons to measure the passage of time. They also determined time by the rising and setting of the Sun. People knew that when the Sun came up in the morning, it was time for a new day.

The rising of the Sun still signals the start of a new day for most people, although midnight is the official start.

A watch or a clock shows us how much time has passed. Nature also displays the results of time passing. People grow older. Little cubs grow into huge bears, and tiny seeds grow into tall trees.

From the use of sundials to the most complicated electric and **atomic clocks**, humans have attempted to keep track of time for centuries. This book explains how people have calculated time over the ages. It also explains how time as we measure it relates to the universe and our solar system. A section at the end of the book answers some common questions about time and provides a timeline that summarizes the history of telling time.

Time and Space

The Big Bang is thought to have taken place about 10 to 15 billion years ago.

When Time Began

Many scientists think that our universe began between 10 and 15 billion years ago with an enormous explosion in space called the **Big Bang**. Our universe is believed to have come into existence at the moment the Big Bang occurred. Space began to expand, and time started to pass.

Billions of years after the Big Bang, our solar system formed. The solar system consists of the Sun, the planets, moons, and other objects such as comets and asteroids. It is part of an even bigger system, a galaxy called the Milky Way. About every 200 million years, the solar system revolves around the center of the galaxy.

This photo shows what a spiral galaxy in the Antlia Constellation looked like long ago. The Milky Way is also a spiral galaxy.

Stars in other galaxies are very far away. It can take billions of years for their light to reach Earth. By the time their light is visible to us, these stars might no longer exist. They may have collapsed or exploded in space.

Although we cannot travel back in time, scientists have found a way for us to look back in time. Using telescopes, astronomers can take pictures of stars whose light has just now reached our solar system. Some of these stars are 12 million **light-years** away. That means we are looking 12 million years into the past.

The Year

By observing the movements of the Sun and other objects in the sky, people began to mark the passing of time. The Sun is at the center of our solar system. It is how we measure time on Earth. The Sun's **gravity** pulls all of the planets around it on **elliptical**, or oval, paths called orbits.

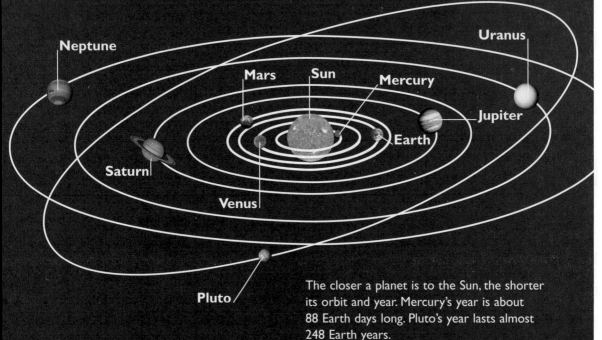

Neptune
Uranus
Mars
Sun
Mercury
Jupiter
Saturn
Earth
Venus
Pluto

The closer a planet is to the Sun, the shorter its orbit and year. Mercury's year is about 88 Earth days long. Pluto's year lasts almost 248 Earth years.

Each planet's year is measured by how long it takes that planet to make one complete orbit of the Sun. This period of time is called the solar year. Earth takes about 365¼ days to orbit the Sun, so Earth's solar year is about 365¼ days long. Calendars today mark most years as only 365 days long. What happens to those extra quarter days? Every four years, one day, February 29, is added to the year. This year is called a leap year.

The Month

Ancient peoples watched the Moon change its shape from a full Moon to a new Moon to a full Moon again. These changes are known as the **phases of the Moon**. The 29½ days it takes for the Moon to go through all of its phases is called a lunar month. The word *lunar* means "of the Moon," and the word *month* comes from the word *moon*. A lunar year consists of twelve lunar months. This adds up to 354 days—eleven days less than a solar year. The solar calendar today uses twelve months, each having twenty-eight to thirty-one days. The longer months cover the additional eleven days that were not included in the lunar year.

Phases of the Moon

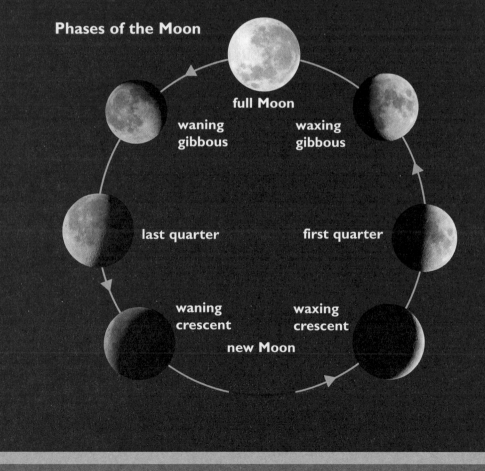

full Moon

waning gibbous

waxing gibbous

last quarter

first quarter

waning crescent

waxing crescent

new Moon

Night and Day

When it is morning in New York, it is night in Melbourne, Australia. This is because Earth spins on its **axis**. As it spins, the side of Earth facing the Sun has daytime. The opposite side has nighttime. Earth takes 24 hours to spin all the way around its axis. People use this time to determine the length of one day.

About 5,000 years ago, the Babylonians divided a day into twenty-four sections. They decided that there would be 60 minutes in an hour and 60 seconds in a minute. People are not sure why the Babylonians used sixty as a base number. Some think it is because sixty is divisible by so many numbers. Others think that it was because the Babylonians thought the number six was important.

daytime in New York

This side of Earth is facing the Sun, so it is daytime there. At the same time, it is night on the other side of Earth because it faces away from the Sun.

nighttime in Melbourne (not visible)

The number of hours of daylight in a day changes over the course of a year. Some days have more hours of daylight than others. It depends on the time of year and location. Earth is tilted on its axis as it orbits the Sun. The number of daylight hours in a particular place is based on the orientation of Earth's tilt. When a hemisphere is tilted away from the Sun, it has fewer hours of daylight. When it is tilted toward the Sun, it has more hours of daylight. When one hemisphere has the most possible hours of daylight and the other has the fewest, it is called a **solstice**. Solstices happen twice a year.

In March and September, both hemispheres have an **equinox**. The equinox is when the Sun is directly over the **equator**. On these days, daylight and nighttime are of equal length throughout the world.

In the polar regions there are times when the Sun does not set at all. This phenomenon is called the Midnight Sun. During these times, children can play soccer long after it would normally be dark in other countries.

The Seasons

People have also used the seasons as a way to measure time during a year. Ancient peoples observed the changes in seasonal weather. In many places, a hot summer leads to a cool autumn. This is followed by a cold winter and then a warm spring. Predictable patterns, repeated year after year, helped people decide when to plant crops or store food for winter.

Not all places on Earth have the same seasons at the same time. As Earth makes its way around the Sun, it rotates around an axis, an imaginary line joining the North Pole, the center of Earth, and the South Pole. The way the axis is tilted determines how strong the Sun's rays are in a particular place at a particular time. It is what causes the seasons.

March 21
It is the spring equinox in the Northern Hemisphere and the autumn equinox in the Southern Hemisphere.

June 21
It is the summer solstice in the Northern Hemisphere and the winter solstice in the Southern Hemisphere.

Sun

September 23
It is the autumn equinox in the Northern Hemisphere and the spring equinox in the Southern Hemisphere.

Hallstatt, Austria

Sydney, Australia

February brings warm weather to Australia and snow to Austria.

It is summer in the Northern Hemisphere when the North Pole is tilted toward the Sun. At the same time, the Southern Hemisphere is tilted away from the Sun and has winter. So, while it is summer in North America and Europe, it is winter in Australia.

As Earth continues its orbit around the Sun, the seasons change. The Northern Hemisphere is tilted away from the Sun and has short winter days, while the Southern Hemisphere has long summer days. How many hours of daylight occur during each day in any place on Earth is determined by where Earth is in its orbit around the Sun.

Some places do not have four distinct seasons. Near the equator, Earth's tilt has little effect on the amount of sunlight. So the seasons there are more often marked by changes in weather patterns, such as the start of a wet season or a dry season, rather than by temperature changes.

December 22
It is the winter solstice in the Northern Hemisphere and the summer solstice in the Southern Hemisphere.

Time Zones

Different places on Earth face the Sun at different times as Earth rotates on its axis. To deal with this difference, the world has been divided into twenty-four separate time zones. Time zones were created in the United States and Canada in the 1880s. Railroad managers realized that their schedules needed a single time standard so cross-country travelers would not become confused by local times in small towns. By 1883, railroad managers in the United States had divided the country into four time zones.

> When it is 7:00 A.M. (07:00) in Toronto, what time is it in Melbourne?

World Time Zone Map

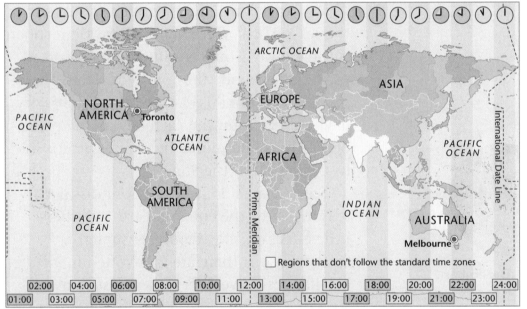

This map shows the world's twenty-four time zones. The time is measured in twenty-four hours, from one midnight to the next. Some large countries are in two time zones and have to choose which time to follow.

In 1884, at an international conference held in Washington, D.C., Earth was divided into twenty-four time zones, with Greenwich, England, serving as the first one, known as the "zero zone."

The lines of **longitude** that divide the time zones run from the North Pole to the South Pole. These imaginary lines are also called **meridians**. Usually, the time zone changes at the meridians, which occur about every 15 degrees. (Here, a degree is a measure of distance, not temperature.) However, sometimes the lines marking different time zones zigzag.

The zero meridian, also called the **Prime Meridian**, marks the center of the zero zone. All clocks are based on the time there, which is called Greenwich Mean Time, or GMT. Moving east of the Prime Meridian, each time zone is one hour later than the previous zone. If it is noon in Greenwich, it is 1:00 P.M. (13:00) in the next time zone to the east. West of the Prime Meridian, each zone is an hour earlier than the one before. If it is noon in Greenwich, it is 11:00 A.M. (11:00) in the first time zone west of Greenwich.

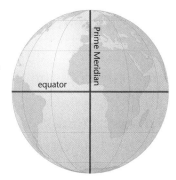

This globe shows the Prime Meridian and the equator. The vertical blue lines are lines of longitude, and the horizontal blue lines are lines of latitude.

The Prime Meridian in Greenwich, England, is marked by an illuminated green line at night.

The International Date Line

When a person travels from one time zone to the next, not only does the time change but sometimes the date changes, too. Once someone travels across the **International Date Line**, the traveler will be in a different day. The International Date Line is located for the most part along the 180 degrees meridian, halfway around the world from the Greenwich meridian. In some places the International Date Line zigzags or bulges. It does this so that small countries can have only one time zone, when a meridian would split the land into two zones.

The last change to the date line was made in 1995 so that all of the Kiribati island group could be in the same day at the same time. Kiribati's Caroline Island is located just west of the date line boundary and so became the first place on Earth to see in the year 2000. It was renamed Millennium Island in 1999 to mark the event.

The International Date Line

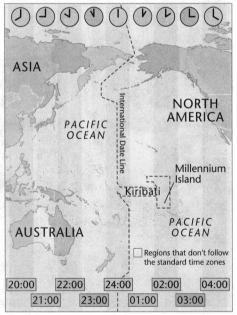

The International Date Line does not run in a straight line. If it did, some countries would experience two days at the same time. You can see more clearly how the date line relates to the world's time zones by looking back at the map on page 82.

Can you find two places on the map that are experiencing different days?

Fred's Journey

Let's follow a traveler named Fred, who is about to leave Hawaii to visit the Philippines. To get to the Philippines, Fred must travel west and cross the International Date Line.

If Fred leaves Hawaii on Tuesday morning, it is already Wednesday in the Philippines. Traveling west across the International Date Line means that he will lose a day.

However, when Fred leaves the Philippines to return to Hawaii, he will have to travel across the International Date Line again. This means that he gains a day. Depending on the time his plane takes off, if he leaves the Philippines on Thursday, he may arrive in Hawaii on Wednesday—the day before he set out!

When Fred crosses the International Date Line, he moves into a new time zone and a new day.

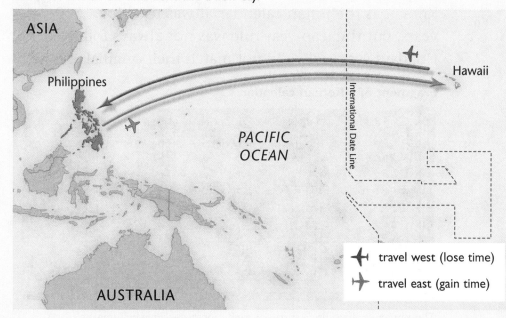

ASIA

Philippines

Hawaii

International Date Line

PACIFIC OCEAN

AUSTRALIA

✈ travel west (lose time)

✈ travel east (gain time)

Measuring Time

Measuring the Year

The first calendars were made to help people remember the dates of events that were important to them. Usually these calendars were based on either lunar year or solar year cycles. After a few years passed, however, these calendars would not match up with the seasons. So, people dropped or added days or months to fit with the cycle of the seasons.

The Romans used a ten-month calendar, which didn't add up to the 365¼ days of the solar year. So they added two months to follow the lunar calendar and also inserted an extra month every other year.

In 46 B.C., the Roman emperor, Julius Caesar, established a solar calendar with twelve months. Known as the Julian calendar, it was used for 1,500 years, but the leap-year rule was not always followed. Holidays eventually did not match their original seasons.

Fragment of a Roman calendar

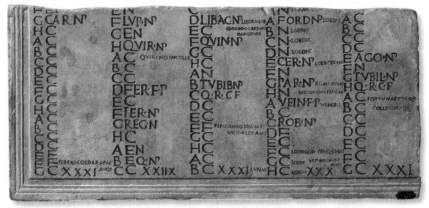

The Romans called the first day of each month *calends*, which means "to call out." This is where our word *calendar* comes from.

The Hebrew calendar is based on both the Sun and the Moon. It is used by Jews worldwide to determine, among other things, the start of the new Hebrew month and when the Jewish holidays are. Every month starts (approximately) on the day of a new Moon.

In 1582, Pope Gregory XIII created a new calendar. First, to balance the calendar with the seasons, he removed ten days. For the first year only, the calendar skipped from October 4 to October 15. This new Gregorian calendar, which added a leap year once every four years, is still in use today.

Another calendar is the Hebrew calendar. It is like the Gregorian calendar, but instead of having a leap year, it has a thirteenth month every few years. This calendar was developed and first used more than 3,000 years ago. That means that the year 2010 would be 5770–5771 on the Hebrew calendar. Other calendars were also developed within the Chinese, Indian, Islamic, Aztec, and Mayan cultures.

The Aztec calendar was based on the Sun. This Aztec calendar stone has the Sun God at its center.

Measuring the Day

Clocks help measure time in much smaller units than calendars. The first timepieces were made about 4,000 years ago. They were not very accurate. The Babylonians were the first to divide daylight time into twelve units of time. No one is exactly sure why the Babylonians chose twelve.

The markings on a sundial show us what time it is.

Objects in sunlight cast shadows of different lengths and at different angles throughout the day. Early clocks that used the Sun used large objects, such as pyramids, or smaller sticks or poles, to cast a shadow that could be tracked. People could tell the time by looking at the shadow's length and angle. This method of telling time led to the invention of sundials by the Babylonians. The shadow cast by a pointer would move across the sundial surface, which was marked with lines to show the hours of the day.

This large structure is the sundial's pointer.

The largest sundial in the world is in Jaipur, India. It is part of an outdoor observatory, which has many giant instruments for watching the sky.

The rising levels of water in a clepsydra's lower container measure the passing of time.

Another type of clepsydra is a single container with a hole from which water escapes. The decreasing levels of water inside measure the passing of time. The one above is from ancient Egypt.

Water clocks were used in ancient Greece and Egypt thousands of years ago. A water clock is also called a **clepsydra** (KLEHP-sih-druh). Unlike sundials, a clepsydra could show the time indoors or at night. Water dripped at a constant rate from one container to another. The markings on the bottom container were used to measure the hours that passed as it filled. One use for clepsydras was to time speeches in law courts.

An hourglass uses sand to measure passing time. It takes one hour for the sand to completely run from the top to the bottom of this hourglass.

The hourglass is another timepiece used thousands of years ago. It was similar to the clepsydra, but it used sand. The sand flowed from one section of a glass container to another. The special shape of the glass allowed sand to pass through at a steady rate. The amount of sand in the bottom of the glass showed how much time had passed.

Mechanical Clocks

The tick-tock sound of a clock was first heard when people started making mechanical clocks. We do not know exactly who invented the first mechanical clocks. Some people believe they were invented in Europe in the late 1200s or early 1300s. Mechanical clocks used weights or springs, which could be easily damaged, so they were not always very accurate.

By the 1500s, people were making small, portable clocks, called pocket watches. These signified a big change in time telling—people could now tell time wherever they were. People were also making other kinds of clocks, and these clocks were often very large. Some were made of iron and weighed several tons.

History of Mechanical Clocks

Salisbury Cathedral clock

seventeenth-century portable clock

pendulum clock

1386	1510	1657
The world's oldest surviving mechanical clock is built at Salisbury Cathedral in southern England. It is still working today.	The first spring-powered clocks are made by Peter Henlein, a German locksmith. They are very light and can be carried easily.	The first pendulum clock is made by Christiaan Huygens, a Dutch astronomer.

About a hundred years later, pendulum clocks were invented. The pendulum swings from left to right in a constant motion. This feature made pendulum clocks more reliable than previous clocks. They were inaccurate by only a few seconds each day.

In 1735, clocks became even more accurate. Until then, it had been especially hard to tell time aboard a ship. The rocking of the ship on the waves interfered with the swings of a clock's pendulum, causing the clock to be inaccurate. This led one man, John Harrison, to invent the first **marine chronometer**. The chronometer worked using a balance spring with two weights. The weights enabled the chronometer to keep accurate time regardless of the rocking of the ship.

Big Ben

traditional cuckoo clock

Harrison 4 marine chronometer

1730	1759	1859
Cuckoo clocks are first used in Germany. Cuckoo clocks use a pendulum and weights to keep time.	John Harrison makes an accurate timekeeper for people at sea. It is his fourth attempt at making one and is called the Harrison 4.	Big Ben is built. It sits atop the Houses of Parliament in London, England. The name at first only referred to the bell that strikes the hour.

Digital Time

Today, many clocks do not have springs or pendulums. They run on electricity or batteries.

Digital clocks have an electronic counter instead of gears, like traditional clocks have. Many also have a very small quartz crystal inside. When powered by a battery, the crystal vibrates. If the clock has hands, the crystal's pulse causes these hands to move. Most of today's watches also use a quartz crystal.

Many electric clocks and watches don't have hands. They have what is called an LCD, a liquid crystal display, or an LED, a light emitting diode. The time is shown in numerals.

LCD

LED

quartz crystal

battery

Digital timepieces were revolutionary when they first appeared in the 1970s, but they are now an everyday sight.

Mechanical clocks are still in use, but most clocks and watches today are electric and don't need to be wound.

The clocks that are most accurate at keeping time are atomic clocks. They don't use a spring, a pendulum, or a quartz crystal. Atomic clocks count the steady vibrations of an **atom**, which is the smallest part of an element. These beats are very dependable. Atoms can vibrate more than 9 billion times a second. Since 1967, atomic clocks have been used to keep the official time throughout the world. It can take millions of years before an atomic clock is inaccurate by even one second.

The future might bring many new ways to measure time. New technology will probably introduce even more accurate clocks and calendars. People will always be running to meet trains, checking to see when a soccer game starts, and listening for the bell to signal the end of a test or some other event. No matter what new timepieces we have, people will still be asking, "What time is it?"

The first atomic clock was made in the United States. It used an ammonia molecule as the source of vibrations.

iOpeners

What Time Is It?

By Susan Ring

DK | Celebration Press
Pearson Learning Group

Apply the Strategy

Activating Background Knowledge Throughout Reading

1. Read pages 72–85. Place sticky notes in the text where you activate background knowledge about a new topic.
2. Record the information in a three-column chart, labeling the columns *New Topics, My Background Knowledge,* and *Source*.

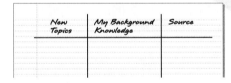

Asking Questions to Fill Gaps in Your Background Knowledge

1. Read pages 86–93. Use sticky notes in one color to mark places where you have questions and in another color to mark where you find the answers.
2. Record information in a three-column chart, labeling the columns *My Questions, Gaps in My Knowledge,* and *Answers/No Answers.*

My Questions	Gaps in My Knowledge	Answers/No Answers

Revising Background Knowledge to Accommodate New Information

1. Read pages 96–97. Think about how some of the new information might change or add to your background knowledge.
2. Record new information in a T-chart, labeling the columns *Topics New to Me* and *Information Added to My Background Knowledge.*

Topics New to Me	Information Added to My Background Knowledge

Questions About Time

Is time travel possible?

There are theories that if we were able to move faster than the speed of light, or could travel through wormholes in space, we might be able to travel back in time. These ideas have been used in many exciting television shows and movies, but many scientists believe that they would be impossible to do. However, it may be that we will understand these things better in the future—only time will tell...

How can you tell which years will be leap years?

Leap years occur in every year that can be divided evenly by four. However, to keep the calendar in line with the time it takes for Earth to orbit the Sun, the only century years that are leap years are those that can be divided by 400.

Why do we need to measure time so precisely?

Many people have jobs that depend on knowing the precise time. For example, a ship's navigator finds longitude by comparing the time on a chronometer with local time.

Timeline of Timekeeping

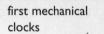

1500 B.C.	early 1300s (A.D.)	1657	1730–1735
sundial used by ancient Egyptians and Greeks	first mechanical clocks	first pendulum clocks	first marine chronometers

How do animals know what time it is?

Well, they can't tell you if it's 4:00 P.M. or 5:00 P.M., but they can tell day from night. They also have a built-in biological clock that tells them when it is time to eat, migrate, build a nest, or watch for their masters to come home from school.

migrating geese

What's a body clock?

A body, or biological, clock is the automatic system in humans and other animals that controls the cycles of sleeping and waking. Your body clock is what wakes you up in the morning and what makes you feel sleepy at night.

How can you tell the time if you don't have a clock?

Some people, such as farmers, spend much of their time outdoors. These people can often tell the time quite accurately without a clock. From long experience, they learn to judge the time from the position of the Sun in the sky. Noon occurs when the Sun reaches its highest point in the sky. Times in the morning and afternoon can be estimated by the angle of the Sun above the horizon.

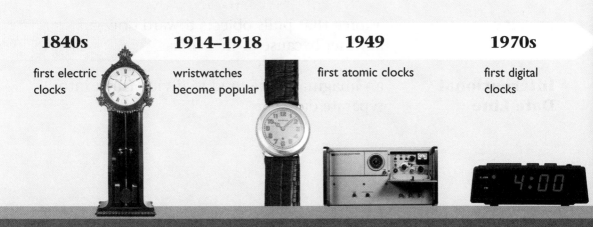

1840s
first electric clocks

1914–1918
wristwatches become popular

1949
first atomic clocks

1970s
first digital clocks

Glossary

atom   the smallest particle of an element

atomic clocks   extremely accurate clocks that use the vibrations of atoms to keep time

axis   an imaginary line running through the center of Earth from the North Pole to the South Pole

Big Bang   the term used to describe the theory on the explosive birth of the universe between 10 and 15 billion years ago

clepsydra   an ancient water clock

elliptical   oval shaped

equator   an imaginary line around Earth that is the same distance from the North and South poles and divides Earth into the Northern and Southern hemispheres

equinox   when the Sun is directly over the equator

gravity   a force that pulls objects toward one another because of their mass

International Date Line   an imaginary line used to divide Earth into separate days

light-year	the distance light travels in one year
longitude	imaginary lines around Earth that run from the North Pole to the South Pole measuring how far east or west a place is on Earth, compared to the Prime Meridian
marine chronometer	a type of clock powered by springs that uses a balance spring and two weights to keep accurate time on a ship at sea
meridians	lines of longitude
phases of the Moon	the different shapes of the sunlit parts of the Moon as seen from Earth during the Moon's 29½ day orbit
Prime Meridian	the imaginary line that runs around Earth from the North Pole to the South Pole, through Greenwich, England, and marks 0 degrees longitude
solstice	when the Sun is overhead at its northernmost and southernmost points in the sky

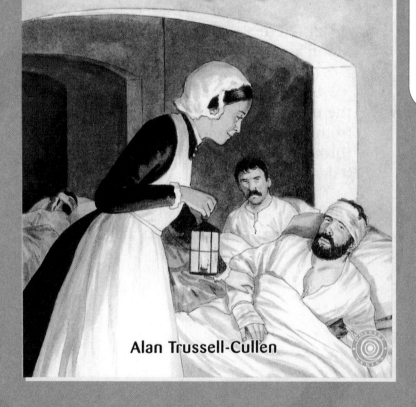

Lady with the Lamp
The Florence Nightingale Story

Alan Trussell-Cullen

Apply the Strategy

Lesson 1

Making Text-to-Self Connections

1. Read pages 103–109. Think about how the events and people in the text relate to your own life.
2. Record your text-to-self connections in a T-chart, labeling the left side *My Text-to-Self Connection* and the right side *How It Helps Me Understand the Text*.
3. Share your connections with a partner.

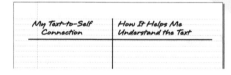

Lesson 2

Making Text-to-Text Connections

1. Skim pages 103–109. Think about ways the text reminds you of other texts you've read.
2. Record your text-to-text connections in a three-column chart, labeling the columns *Other Text I've Read, My Connection,* and *How It Helps Me Understand the Text*.

3. Share your connections with a partner.

Other Text I've Read	My Connection	How It Helps Me Understand the Text

Lesson 3

Making Text-to-World Connections

1. Read pages 110–115. Think about how the text links to places or things you know about but haven't experienced.
2. Record your text-to-world connections in a T-chart, labeling the left side *My Text-to-World Connection* and the right side *How It Helps Me Understand the Text.*
3. Share your connections with a partner.

Table of Contents

Chapter One
A Girl with Nothing to Do

On May 12, 1820, an Englishwoman gave birth to a little girl in the beautiful city of Florence, Italy. The woman and her husband thought their baby daughter was as beautiful as the city itself, so they named her Florence—Florence Nightingale.

Florence's parents were very rich. As Florence grew up in London, her family was able to give her everything she needed. Her mother expected her to do what other rich English girls did— they were expected to visit friends and go to parties and eventually marry a rich young man. Rich girls certainly weren't expected to work or have jobs.

But Florence wasn't like the other rich girls. At sixteen, she decided she wanted to spend her life doing things to help others. There were many sick people who lived near their home in England. Florence started visiting sick people and bringing them food and medicine.

Her parents thought this was all right, but when she asked if she could go to learn how to be a nurse at a nearby hospital, they were horrified. Hospitals in

those days were crowded places. They were dirty and smelly. The nurses who worked there were poorly educated and knew very little about caring for people. Florence's parents didn't want her to be around those kinds of people.

But what was even more shocking for Florence's parents was the idea that their daughter wanted to *work*! Rich girls didn't have jobs in those days.

Her family sent Florence on a trip to Europe to try to make her forget these ideas. But this only made Florence all the more determined to become a nurse.

While traveling through Germany, she visited the Kaiserwerth Institute, which had a good hospital and was one of the few places where nurses could be trained. Florence went back to England and begged her father to let her go to the

Kaiserwerth Institute to study and learn to be a nurse. At first, everyone in her family was furious. But finally, in 1851, her father gave in.

Chapter Two

A Nurse at Last

All the people at the Kaiserwerth Institute had devoted their lives to helping others. There was a hospital for sick people, schools, and an orphanage for homeless children. The work was very hard. Florence had to get up each morning at five o'clock, and she worked all day and long into the night. But she loved it.

"I am as happy as the day is long!" she wrote in her diary.

After her training, Florence returned to London, where she was determined to put her nurse's training to work. She took charge of nursing at a number of hospitals. But in 1854 there was an outbreak of cholera. This terrible disease is very easy to catch, and it spreads very quickly. In those days, many people died of cholera. The nearby Middlesex Hospital was full of people who were sick and dying of the disease. Florence didn't hesitate. She took charge of the hospital and did everything she could for the patients.

It was good training for what was to be the next and greatest challenge of her life.

Chapter Three
War Breaks Out

In March, 1854, war broke out in Crimea between Russia and Turkey. A year later, Britain and France joined Turkey in the battle against the Russians. But the war went badly, and soon there were many sick and wounded soldiers.

They were taken to a hospital in Scutari, Turkey.

Conditions in the hospital were appalling. There were no nurses to help the doctors. The doctors were not only trying to help the soldiers who had been wounded in battle, but they were also doing what they could for soldiers who were sick and dying of terrible diseases like cholera and typhus. Five out of every six soldiers who died in the Scutari Hospital died of these diseases rather than their battle wounds.

"This is not right!" thundered Florence, when she read in the newspapers about the suffering of the soldiers in Crimea. She sat down to write a letter to Sir Sidney Herbert, an old friend in the government. She offered to take charge of the nursing in Crimea.

At exactly the same time, Sir Sidney was writing a letter to *her*, begging her to come and help!

Florence sprang into action. She quickly gathered a group of 38 nurses and set sail for Scutari.

When she arrived, she was horrified. The hospital was filthy. There was hardly any clean water, and bandages and medical supplies were scarce. Much of the food was unfit to eat. There were sick and dying soldiers everywhere, and more arrived each day. The army doctors were not able to cope.

At first, army officers and doctors resented Florence. They didn't believe women could do this kind of work. They tried to keep her and her nurses out of the hospital.

"How could a group of women possibly

help here? Just go home to England and do your embroidery!" they said.

"We'll wait for you to change your mind," said Florence. And they waited.

More and more sick and wounded soldiers began to arrive in the already overcrowded hospital. Finally, the army officers and doctors turned to Florence.

"Please, will you help?" they said.

Immediately, Florence and her team went to work. Florence had noticed that fewer people died in hospitals when conditions were cleaner and there was fresh water available.

They brought fresh water in and cleaned the hospital from top to bottom. They nursed the patients and dressed their wounds. Fewer soldiers caught diseases like dysentery, cholera, and typhus, which spread easily. Florence and her nurses washed all the clothing and bedding. They cooked good food to help the sick recover. They worked tirelessly.

Florence hardly had any time to sleep. She wrote letters home for the soldiers who couldn't write, and at night she walked through every ward of the hospital. She carried a lamp with her, and she said goodnight to every single person. The soldiers came to love her. They called her the Lady with the Lamp.

In those days, news traveled very slowly. But in time, word of Florence's work reached England, and soon the newspapers were singing the praises of Florence Nightingale and her nurses. She had become a national hero!

Making Inferences
Great Readers Use What They Know

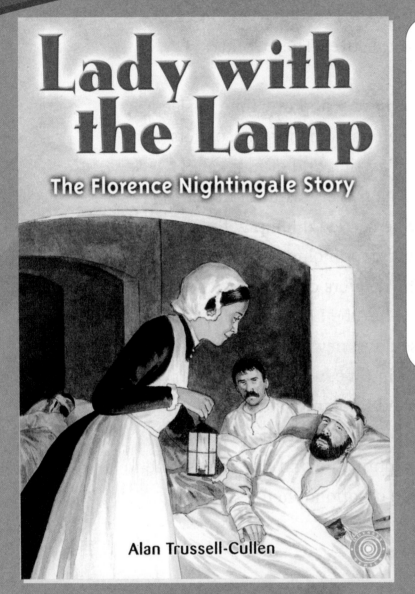

Lady with the Lamp

The Florence Nightingale Story

Alan Trussell-Cullen

Words to Know

committee (p. 119): "a group of people selected to take action on a matter"

establishment (p. 120): "bringing into existence"

equipped (p. 119): "having necessary supplies"

humble (p. 123): "modest"

principles (p. 120): "rules of conduct"

shunned (p. 122): "avoided"

Apply the Strategy

Lesson 1

Using What You Know to Make Inferences

1. Read pages 118–119, and stop after the third paragraph on page 119. Use what you know and clues in the text to make inferences.
2. Record information in a three-column chart, labeling the columns *Text Clues, Background Knowledge,* and *My Inference.*

Text Clues	Background Knowledge	My Inference

Lesson 2

Using Inferences to Clarify Words and Concepts

1. Begin reading the last paragraph on page 119. Stop before the last paragraph on page 122. Think about how using inferences can help you clarify text that you find confusing.
2. Record your inferences in a three-column chart, labeling the columns *What Confuses Me, Clues That Help to Make an Inference,* and *My Inference.*

What Confuses Me	Clues That Help to Make an Inference	My Inference

Lesson 3

Revising and Expanding Inferences as You Read

1. Begin with the last paragraph on page 122 and read through page 124. Think about your inferences and how you might revise or expand on them as you read new information.
2. Record revised or expanded inferences in a three-column chart, labeling the columns *My Inference, New Information,* and *My Revised/Expanded Inference.*

My Inference	New Information	My Revised/Expanded Inference

Chapter Four
The Nightingale Nurses

In 1856, the war in Crimea came to an end, and Florence returned to England. She was surprised to find how famous she had become. She didn't like all the fuss people were making about her.

"There is still so much that needs to be

done," she said.

Queen Victoria invited Florence to Scotland for a vacation. Florence accepted, but not because she wanted a vacation. She took the opportunity to tell the queen about all the changes that hospitals needed to make.

The queen listened carefully. Afterward, she set up a special committee to look at the way army hospitals were run. Florence was delighted. She wrote a long report for the committee, describing everything that needed to change.

But Florence wanted to change the way ordinary hospitals were run, too. "Hospitals have to be clean, well-organized, and better equipped. Nurses need to be educated and well-trained," she declared.

One of the ways Florence helped make changes was by writing letters.

She loved writing letters. She wrote to everyone she thought might help make a difference. She even wrote the first textbook for nurses, *Notes on Nursing: What It Is and What It Is Not.*

Florence continued to write letters, but her dream was to have a training school for nurses, where women could be taught how to properly take care of the sick and injured. That dream finally came true in 1860 with the establishment of the Nightingale School of Nursing, in London.

Many people gave money to help start the school, which was founded on Florence's ideas and principles. She took a personal interest in all the nurses and gave each one a gift when they finished their training.

The probationer nurses, as they were called, attended the training program for

NIGHTINGALE SCHOOL OF NURSING

a year. They dressed in plain brown uniforms and lived in a wing of Saint Thomas's Hospital, in London. All their living expenses were paid, and each received an additional allowance of £10 a year (about $50). The training for the nurses was very practical. Nurses learned how to make hospital beds, how to change dressings, and how to help doctors care for patients.

The school was to provide the foundation for the way nurses are trained, not only in England, but around the world.

Despite her fame, Florence shunned public events. She preferred to help people in a quiet way. When she returned from the Crimean War, for example, she brought back a number of homeless children and soldiers, including a one-legged sailor boy and a terribly scarred Russian soldier. Florence supported them all for the rest of her life.

The people she helped did not forget her. The city of London gave her the Freedom of the City of London award. In 1907, King Edward awarded her the Order of Merit. This is a very special award, and Florence was the first woman ever to receive it. When she died, people wanted her to be buried in Westminster Abbey alongside all the kings and queens and the country's most famous people. But in her will, Florence insisted that she be buried with her family. This famous woman, who saved thousands of lives and completely changed the way sick people are nursed and cared for around the world, remained humble and modest to the end. As she requested, all it says on her grave is: *F.N. Born 1820, Died 1910.*

The first training school for nurses in the United States was established in 1870 in Boston, and the first nurse to qualify was Linda Richards. In 1877, Linda traveled to England to continue her studies at Saint Thomas's Hospital, where she met Florence Nightingale. In time, she helped set up a number of nurse training schools in the United States and Japan.